Are You Arresting Your Blessing?

Are you waiting on God or is God waiting on you?

By Melissa Weathersby

PRESS

Printed in the United States of America

ISBN 9781613795385

www.xulonpress.com

This book is dedicated to all of the people who are waiting on their promise from God. My heart's desire is that you hang on to every God-inspired dream and never let go until you see the fullness of His love for you.

www.greatlighthouse.com

ar·rest [uh-rest]

noun

**An act of stopping or the state
of being stopped**

(Dictionary.com)

Table of Contents

Introduction

Blessed to Be a Blessing

What is a blessing?

Is it wealth? Is it fame? Is it the freedom to do whatever you want, how you want, and where you want? Dictionary.com defines *blessing* as "the invoking of God's favor upon a person" or "a favor or gift bestowed by God, thereby bringing happiness." Nowhere does the definition mention material possessions or gain. Is it possible that we have moved away from what God originally intended when He promised to bless us? Is it possible that in our quest for more *things*, we have lost focus on what God is trying to do in our lives?

To receive God's favor is greater than any material gain we might achieve. There is nothing more complete and beneficial than God's favor. "What is favor?" you may ask. *Favor* is defined as "the state of being approved or held in regard," or "excessive kindness or unfair partiality; preferential treatment" (Dictionary.com). How would your life be different if God began to show you excessive kindness or preferential treatment? How would your life change if you knew you were approved and held in high regard by the most-high God, and He began to show you preferential treatment everywhere your feet trod? I dare to say your life would be transformed into something people would take notice of, and they would begin to watch your life and want what you have—the favor and blessing of the Lord!

In this book, I want to help you unlock your life so that your blessings can be released and overflow and impact everything and everyone around you. Let me start by sharing some background information.

I felt impressed to write this book while I was in the midst of a severe wilderness experience. I was at a major crossroad and was very unsure of which direction to take. Everything that I did seemed to just bottom out. My businesses had dried up, although everyone around me continued to enjoy prosperity. People in my life who had once been reliable and dependable became flaky or disappeared. The dreams and visions I had treasured in my heart shriveled up, and it became harder and harder for me to hear from the Lord.

I have always been a very ambitious and industrious person. I was extremely goal oriented and achievement focused, and most of what I set my mind and will to do happened. It wasn't always easy or fun, but I generally got whatever I put my mind to. I was in management positions before I was twenty-five years old. I completed a graduate degree by the time I was twenty-eight. I owned two businesses by the time I was twenty-nine. I was definitely someone who could hold her own, and adversity just seemed to fuel my effort. If I wanted something, there wasn't much that could stand in my way.

At the beginning of my wilderness experience, I decided that a move away from my hometown was necessary and relocated to what I perceived as a glamorous city in northern Texas. I was definitely ready to take my earnings and Rolodex to the next level. Little did I know that the Lord was about to put the emergency brake on my plans and take me on an unexpected detour to freedom, with blessings that would surpass my every imagination. The process was full of pain and conflict about what I had come to believe during my Christian walk, but it was absolutely necessary in order for me to live the life the Lord was calling me to.

This is not a "name it and claim it" book. Neither is it a book about spiritual warfare or generational curses that oppose the blessings of the Lord for believers. This book offers biblical insight regarding the order of the Lord and the things we may be doing that block—or arrest—our blessings. God's Word tells us, "My people are destroyed from lack of knowledge" (Hos. 4:6). And although His Word never changes and God does not lie, we are often complacent and lethargic about living out His instructions through His Word.

This book will uncover what I believe to be key principles to unlocking your blessings—the blessings that the Lord is longing to give to you. He wants all of His children to live healthy, prosperous, and abundant lives so that they can be examples to the world and have the ability to bless others. It is my hope and prayer that you will allow the Holy Spirit to minister to you as you read this book and let Him to expose any areas in your life that may be hindering God's best for you.

Life Talk

My personal relationship with Jesus began when I was born again as a high school senior after years of living in rigid, traditional religion. My earlier experience with religion was not positive; however, I never realized that until I began to learn more about God's Word and discovered that I had missed the big picture. From my perspective, my religious upbringing taught me that I was a lowly sinner, that Jesus died for me because of my rebellious and sinful nature, and that I should be eternally fearful of His judgment because nothing I did would ever be good enough. I was destined to do repetitive, formulated prayers in order to have any hope of entering heaven, in addition to praying to dead saints and dead people who were possibly better than me and had better access to God's throne.

I was forever on my knees, staring up at a crucifix—not an empty cross—that displayed His broken, bleeding body and was continually reminded of how worthless I was and that I would have to do many good works and pray the trillions of prayers in order to be accepted into His kingdom. I was firmly rooted in fear, guilt, condemnation, and intimidation.

On one hand, the good news is that I learned about God the Father, God the Son, and God the Holy Spirit. But on the other hand, I learned about them only in pieces and parts, not in any manner that fully allowed me to know their persons or their personalities. *I just knew that I was on my way to hell unless I could be perfect and flawless.*

With this mentality, I found it extremely difficult to receive God's love and salvation. I constantly struggled to battle that "being good" or "being better than so-and-so" mind-set that would rise up and challenge me to work harder so that I could at least earn entry into heaven and possibly even a higher seat. Salvation was something to earn or strive for, not something as simple as saying, "Yes, Lord. I am a sinner, but I repent. Jesus, come into my life and be my Lord." Little did I know that my works mentality would hinder me from receiving many miracles and blessings God had in store for me.

We have heard it before: "The mind is the battle-field," or "As a man thinketh, so he is." Not realizing that my faulty perspective about my relationship with God had everything to do with the level of access I had to my blessings, I struggled to learn a very difficult—yet very important—lesson: when your foundation is works-based and achievement oriented, it is difficult to build a house that can withstand the winds and rains of life. And when things began to unravel in my life, I indeed found it difficult to believe or trust that the Lord could love me in my "lowly state." But hallelujah for revelation, knowledge, and good, solid teaching! Our God is always on time, and He is always in the details.

Key #1

Faith

"And without faith it is impossible to please God, because anyone who comes to him must believe that he exists and that he rewards those who earnestly seek him." Hebrews 11:6

D o you really believe that God exists? I bet that most of you reading this book would answer (or shout) an emphatic "Yes!" to this question. But it is the second part of this verse that needs to be fully received: "he *rewards* those who *earnestly* seek him" (emphasis mine).

The dictionary defines *earnestly* as "serious in intention, purpose, or effort; sincerely zealous." To be earnest about seeking God, then, means that you give *serious* attention and effort to seeking Him, even when things begin to unravel or feel increasingly uncomfortable. Even when you are being pressed on all sides and there seems to be no way of escape, you seek Him. Even when hell is raging against you and everything in your life that has meaning—your body, your mind, your marriage, your children, your loved ones, your career—you still seek Him. Being serious in your pursuit means letting go of anyone or anything that stands between you and God's will for your life or circumstances. Are you serious enough to make up your mind that if He said it, that settles it, and nothing can shake you loose from His promise—period, no other options?

But what exactly is faith, as spoken of in our verse above? A few verses earlier, in Hebrews 11:1, the Bible says, "Now faith is *confidence* in what we hope for and *assurance* about what we do not see" (emphasis mine). Confidence and assurance are what God desires from His creation. If you are fully confident that God is your all-in-all and is who His Word says He is, then you *will* be assured that every promise and every plan for your life will come to pass.

But *fully confident* is much more than a feeling or a great idea. Being fully confident is a level that many people continue to wrestle with. It transcends any emotion or thought. It is the complete, bold, unshakable, and immovable belief that what you hope for is what God has in store for you, and you will be committed to your belief regardless of what you see, think, or feel.

Is this easy? Is this something that every believer automatically possesses without any effort? Absolutely not! It has been my experience that trials and tests increase our faith, just as lifting weights develops and sculpts beautiful and effective muscles. If we are not fit, we cannot pick up hundred-pound weights and begin to do repeated lifts. Not only do we have to condition our bodies to lifting the weight, but we have to learn how to properly stand and hold the weights in order to prevent serious injury. People have sustained serious, even fatal, injuries while trying to lift weights carelessly or lift weights they were not prepared to carry.

In similar fashion, the Lord will use the trials of life to help us develop our trust in Him, which invariably increases our faith. The more complex or lengthy the trial, the stronger we become after the test is complete. It took me a long time to stop trying to fight this process or skip steps in what I thought was torture or a setback. In reality, those uncomfortable lessons were preparing me to trust Him more and more. And I found that, over time, I was even able to stand in the gap for other people with lesser faith and carry them into a new realm of belief as God worked out situations in their lives.

I have discovered that with every victory I attain, my faith increases again. I know now that my faith pleases God, and He will reward me for having confidence and assurance in His plan for my life.

If you struggle in this area, know that you are not alone. Many believers waver when trials start pounding against them. In those times, it is absolutely vital to stand on God's Word and His promises for your life. Knowing what His Word says about your situation is important. Read the Word daily, and make it a habit to study what you read (see Matthew 7:24–27.) Don't just skim the chapters and feel like you've done your part. God desires you to know Him on a deeper, more personal level, so skimming and skimping isn't going to cut it. Remember, you will always reap what you sow (Gal. 6:7–8). If you sow mediocrity, you will reap mediocrity.

Another tendency we have as believers is to want everything instantaneously and then give up when we think enough time has passed. We end up throwing away our faith when what we prayed for doesn't happen right away. However, Ecclesiastes 3:1–8 tells us that there is a time for everything. So be patient, and continue to believe while you are waiting for God to act. Remember, it is impossible to please God without faith. A delay in getting your answer does not mean a denial, so continue to believe.

Remember Abraham and Sarah? They waited for Isaac for twenty-five years—that's two and a half decades! It's no wonder Sarah laughed the final time the angel showed up to confirm God's promise to her and Abraham (Gen. 18:12; read Genesis 18:1-19 for understanding). Maybe some of you are laughing right now at what you perceive to be a dead dream or promise, but you had better be ready for what God says is yours! He is never late, and He is always, always on time!

Some of you are not prepared for what God is about to do, so He is waiting on you to get your act together. Do you have unresolved issues? What about some unfinished business? Tie up your loose ends and see if your blessings don't arrive seemingly overnight. Once you have your affairs cleaned up and all your loose ends cut and tied, *expect* God to move.

Hebrews 10:35–37 says, "So do not throw away your confidence; it will be richly rewarded. You need to persevere so that when you have done the will of God, you will receive what he has promised." Stand on His Word! He will deliver what

He has promised if you will anchor yourself and do what you are supposed to be doing. Walk the straight line, never give up, and keep expecting! Do you know what perseverance means? It means to have "steady persistence in a course of action, a purpose, a state, etc., especially in spite of difficulties, obstacles, or discouragement"! Being persistent requires you to be stubborn and obstinate about your belief. You *will* receive your blessing if you don't give up or give in.

Some believers do ask and pray, yet secretly they believe that God cannot do anything (or will not do anything) about their situation. They doubt God's ability or desire to manifest blessings in their lives or on their behalf. This is an area that must be healed. As James 1:6 teaches us, "But when you ask, you must believe and not doubt, because the one who doubts is like a wave of the sea, blown and tossed by the wind."

Some of you may already feel blown and tossed about, so check your heart and really search yourself to find out if you truly believe that God can do what He says He can do. Some of you have been so wounded and led astray that you doubt God really loves you enough to bless you or your family. Though I understand that sentiment, I have come to understand that what matters to us matters to Him. If our hearts are heavy, He wants to give us liberty. When we are tossed by the storms of life, He desires to give us peace (Phil. 4:6–9). But we must trust Him and know that He wants us to live in a blessed atmosphere.

The apostle John said, "Beloved, I wish above all things that thou mayest prosper and be in good health, even as thy soul prospereth" (3 John 1:2, KJV). It is safe to assume that most of our blessings are released and then manifested in the natural as our souls prosper. Our souls cannot prosper, however, if we are operating in mind-sets that oppose God's Word.

You might say, "Oh, I don't doubt God's Word," yet you are not *doing* what the Word instructs you to do. Your faith without works is dead (James 2:17). And just as true, your works without faith are dead. You must believe in order to receive. It really is *that* simple!

Some believers are marching around and confessing the promises of God without putting any action to their words. You must *do* something in addition to just confessing words. Are you believing for a job? Get out and apply at the places you want to work. Are you believing for more money? Take a class on financial management. Are you believing for a spouse? Stop sitting at home alone, and get out and be personable and available. How can you be found if you are home alone? Are you believing for good health? Join a gym, get a personal trainer, learn about proper nutrition, cook healthy meals, drink plenty of water, get adequate sleep, stop smoking or putting other unhealthy chemicals into your temple, and make healthy living a priority. Put some action behind your petitions!

Although applied action is necessary to release your blessings, be aware that it is not you who creates the blessing. God and God alone is the one who blesses. Deuteronomy 8:17–20 gives us a warning:

You may say to yourself, "My power and the strength of my hands have produced this wealth for me." But remember the LORD your God, for it is he who gives you the ability to produce wealth, and so confirms his covenant, which he swore to your ancestors, as it is today.

If you ever forget the LORD your God and follow other gods and worship and bow down to them, I testify against you today that you will surely be destroyed. Like the nations the LORD destroyed before you, so you will be destroyed for not obeying the LORD your God.

Never forget who gives the blessings. Honor God, and acknowledge Him in all things.

The prophet Daniel gave King Nebuchadnezzar a similar warning about his prideful behavior (Dan. 4:19–27), yet he chose to continue believing his prosperity was due to the works of his own hands. As a result, he spent seven years wandering around like a beast of the field until he acknowledged where his blessings came from. Once he repented, his mind and his kingdom were restored (Dan. 4:28–37). Remain humble, obedient, and trusting, and then watch once-unavailable doors open for you!

Life Talk

Key #1: Faith

New beginnings can be difficult to grasp no matter how exciting or better they may be than where you are today. When God is bringing us into a new area or new season of change, we sometimes have a tendency to want to continue doing things the "old way" or thinking "old thoughts", about certain situations. It is important to develop a "new attitude" when entering a new season. There may be some old habits, friendships, relationships, locations, etc. that you will have to leave behind. They will not be beneficial or good for your new place, level, or position. It may be uncomfortable at first, but learning how to let go of the old and embracing the new will help you reach the levels that God is taking you to. Not everyone is meant to get to the top with you. Remember Joshua!

It is important to follow God when He is leading you into a new season, and have the faith that it is for your benefit and for your good. Faith and belief are two separate things. Belief is passive while faith is active. Action is required to activate your faith. The Scripture says "faith by itself, if it is not accompanied by action, is dead" (James 2:17); therefore, align your goals with faith and an action plan. Discussing your plans yet doing nothing will not bring the reward that is stored up for you. If you are believing for something, continue to work towards it each day until you see it come to pass. Your faith is pleasing to God! If you do what you **can** do, God will do what you **cannot** do.

Key #2

Obedience

Deuteronomy 28 gives us a complete description of our blessings if we will obey the instruction of the Lord:

If you fully obey the LORD your God and carefully follow all his commands I give you today, the LORD your God will set you high above all the nations on earth. All these blessings will come on you and accompany you if you obey the LORD your God:

You will be blessed in the city and blessed in the country.

The fruit of your womb will be blessed, and the crops of your land and the young of your livestock—the calves of your herds and the lambs of your flocks.

Your basket and your kneading trough will be blessed. You will be blessed when you come in and blessed when you go out.

The LORD will grant that the enemies who rise up against you will be defeated before you. They will come at you from one direction but flee from you in seven.

The LORD will send a blessing on your barns and on everything you put your hand to. The LORD your God will bless you in the land he is giving you.

The LORD will establish you as his holy people, as he promised you on oath, if you keep the commands of the LORD your God and walk in obedience to him. Then all the peoples on earth will see that you are called by the name of the LORD, and they will fear you. The LORD will grant you abundant prosperity—in the fruit of your womb, the young of your livestock and the crops of your ground—in the land he swore to your ancestors to give you.

The LORD will open the heavens, the storehouse of his bounty, to send rain on your land in season and to bless all the work of your hands. You will lend to many nations but will borrow from none. The LORD will make you the head, not the tail. If you pay attention to the commands of the LORD your God that I give you this day and carefully follow them, you will always be at the top, never at the bottom. Do not turn aside from any of the commands I give you today, to the right or to the left, following other gods and serving them.

—DEUTERONOMY 28:1–14

Wow! Meditate on this Scripture passage, and immerse yourself in the fullness of God's desire to bless you. He *wants* to bless you. And your home. And your land. And your children. And your animals. And your pantry. The list goes on and on! God's desire is to bless you and not harm you.

Jeremiah 29:11–13 speaks clearly of this: 'For I know the plans I have for you,' declares the LORD, 'plans to prosper you and not to harm you, plans to give you hope and a future. Then you will call on me and come and pray to me, and I will listen to you. You will seek me and find me when you seek me with all your heart.'

Our task is to seek God with everything that is within us in order to discover His will for our lives. This may involve fasting or having a retreat away from any distractions in order to hear His voice and discern His direction. It is very easy to let the people we admire most dictate the paths we decide to travel. Most of the time, we put those people first and God second. Then we have a meltdown because we are bursting with internal conflicts stemming from our effort to please both people and God. It won't work.

Even if you manage to play this game for a while, your insides will end up feeling like shredded wheat because of the stress you are putting on yourself. When you are living in conflict—especially going against the call of God on your life—

you can be sure that you will suffer something in your flesh. It may be agitation, restlessness, or feeling disconnected from life. You may even develop serious health problems related to the stress of disobedience.

Becoming who God wants you to be takes some heavy self-analysis and disciplined focus. It also takes courage. God told Joshua to be very strong and courageous on his journey into the Promised Land (Josh. 1:9). As the newly appointed leader of the Israelites, he had to lead a people that continued to murmur and complain about their journey even after Moses died. How many of you are surrounded by the same type of people? It may be time for you to let go or distance yourself from relationships and habits that are keeping you from your authentic, God-inspired design. How can God pour out His favor if you refuse to do the things He has created you to do, or if you continually choose to walk away from the places where your blessings reside?

Let's look at the Israelites. A twelve-day trip took them forty years to complete—and only three of the original group of travelers ever saw what had been promised to them. If we study their journey, we can see where their blessings were arrested: (1) they didn't want to listen to Moses and leave Egypt, even though they were in bondage there (Ex. 6:6–9); (2) they didn't value the daily provision of manna that God so graciously provided them (Ex. 16:2); and (3) they never stopped murmuring and complaining during their entire journey to the Promised Land.

If you are constantly speaking words of doubt, making condescending and critical remarks, and complaining about the season you're in, you are probably arresting the blessings God has for you. You will not receive all that He has for you if you continue to live a negative and ungrateful life. You must decide to be at peace with where you are in your life as He leads you through your own wilderness. If you don't, you—like the Israelites—will continue to go around the same mountain repeatedly until you stop going *against* God and start going *with* God. It would be a tragedy to lose out on God's provision because of a sour attitude.

Some believers have fallen into the trap of believing that tithing and offerings take precedence over being obedient and following God's instruction. Scripture tells us that to obey is better than sacrifice. Obedience is the key to open doors, and disobedience keeps doors closed and paths crooked. Take inventory of your habits and actions. Make it your utmost priority to do what God says to do instead of relying on things that you are "giving up" or "sacrificing" in the name of being a "good Christian".

God is looking for *doers* of His Word. Learn to trust His voice and to speedily follow His instruction. According to 1 Samuel 15:22, it is better to do what God tells you to do rather than try to satisfy God with works and sacrifices that you decide are good or necessary. "But Samuel replied: 'Does the LORD delight in burnt offerings and sacrifices as much as in obeying the LORD? To obey is better than sacrifice, and to heed is better than the fat of rams.' "

Life Talk

Key #2 - Blessings for Obedience

When the Lord began getting my attention, I was completely clueless as to what was going on. I had always been successful by the world's standards and was unable to hear with spiritual ears due to the pace I was maintaining. I rarely spent any quiet time with Him, and I was on full-tilt in pursuing material gain and recognition. My environment was an intoxicating mix of glamour, greed, and indulgence, and I was chasing what I thought would give me the freedom to live the life-style I wanted to live. Once my businesses dried up, I realized that I had to do something. That something *meant taking account of what my life had become and then allowing God to recalibrate my existence. For eleven months, I sought work and was repeatedly told I was "over-qualified." I was rejected numerous times and eventually got a county job. That steady paycheck allowed me to pay my rent and bills on time and get back on my feet. It was difficult to get re-acclimated in an environment that had set hours and procedures. I was miserable and grateful all at once! I was learning what submitting to "the harness of the Lord" meant. I could not go until He said to go. I had to learn to be led, which felt like torture to my highly-ambitious, works-based personality! Every time I tried to do things my way, I got another trip around the mountain (i.e. unexpected car repairs, watching my Realtor friends close high dollar deals while I worked at the county, watching office politics play out while I got overlooked, etc.).*

I call those days my "Humble Pie" days. I lived on a diet of Humble Pie until I figured out that God was showing me not to do things my own way. Being obedient to His voice and His direction led me out of the desert and into a land that is now flowing with abundance. I would have never gotten this far if I hadn't made up my mind to just stop trying to do things my way and surrender to His will. I got very serious about listening to numerous ministry messages in order to nourish my spirit so that I could fill up on God's Word. The more I filled my mind and heart with God's Word and prom-

ises, the more excited I became about following His instructions. Without obedience, God's hands are tied, and He is unable to pour out His blessings because His blessings come with purpose. If your purposes are not aligned with His purposes, you are limited in what you will be able to receive. Know that you will be blessed beyond measure if you are walking in obedience to the plans and purposes He has for your life!

Key #3

Words

C onfessing God's Word and speaking what He says about our circumstances has the power to change any atmosphere. The Scriptures declare, "The tongue has the power of life and death, and those who love it will eat its fruit" (Prov. 18:21). In other words, if you love to talk, you will eat the fruit of the words your mouth produces, whether good or bad.

Many believers have not realized their creative power in this area. Do you realize that you have the power to create your atmosphere and circumstances with your words? But first, what does this word *power* mean? According to Dictionary.com, one definition of *power* is "legal ability, capacity, or authority." Wow! If we translate Proverbs 18:21 using the dictionary definition, we could say the tongue has the legal ability, capacity, or authority of life and death, and those who love it will eat the fruit it produces. Please take the time to reread this as many times as necessary in order to comprehend what your words can do. They can actually grow and develop people (including yourself), or they can tear them down and murder them. Remember, you have the legal ability, capacity, or authority to speak life or death with your words, and you will partake of the fruit that your tongue produces. The Bible declares that we should choose life (see Deuteronomy 30:19). Proverbs 18:20 teaches us that "from the fruit of his mouth a man's stomach is filled; with the harvest from his lips he is satisfied." If you are not satisfied with where you are in life, closely examine what you spend your time talking about.

What things have you been saying about your circumstances? "My children are out of control." "I will always be broke. I'm just no good with money." "I will never lose weight." "I can't stop smoking [drinking, indulging, and so forth]." "I can't forgive so-and-so." And on and on and on it goes. Don't forget, you will eat the fruit of your words.

If you have spoken death over your circumstances and over your life, there is still hope. Our God is a God of redemption and resurrection, and you can be redeemed. Begin to declare and decree God's Word over your life. Remember and meditate upon Hebrews 10:23. Reverse the curse of doubt and condemnation about your circumstances. Confess this error of negative words to God and ask Him to forgive your doubt and unbelief, and then continue to speak His Word over your situation.

Don't agree with the things that you merely feel or see. Continue to speak *to* your mountain and not *about* your mountain. Jesus said, "Truly I tell you, if you have faith as small as a mustard seed, you can say to this mountain, 'Move from here to there,' and it will move. Nothing will be impossible for you" (Matt. 17:20). He didn't say, "If you discuss your mountain, it will move"; or

"If you ignore your mountain, it will move"; or "If you think about your mountain, it will move." No, He said, "If you have faith as small as a mustard seed, you can *say* to this mountain, 'Move from here to there,' and it will move. *Nothing* will be impossible for you" (emphasis mine). Don't you see? It's time to start speaking to some of the hindrances in your life and telling them where to go!

Let's consider Elijah's example. For three years, Samaria had been experiencing a severe drought and famine. Elijah had just confirmed God's mighty hand at Mount Carmel. After the Lord displayed Himself to several hundred prophets of Baal, Elijah had the following exchange with King Ahab:

> And Elijah said to Ahab, "Go, eat and drink, for there is the sound of a heavy rain." So Ahab went off to eat and drink, but Elijah climbed to the top of Carmel, bent down to the ground and put his face between his knees.

"Go and look toward the sea," he told his servant. And he went up and looked.

"There is nothing there," he said.

Seven times Elijah said, "Go back."

The seventh time the servant reported, "A cloud as small as a man's hand is rising from the sea."

So Elijah said, "Go and tell Ahab, 'Hitch up your chariot and go down before the rain stops you.'"

Meanwhile, the sky grew black with clouds, the wind rose, a heavy rain came on and Ahab rode off to Jezreel. The power of the LORD came upon Elijah and, tucking his cloak into his belt, he ran ahead of Ahab all the way to Jezreel.

—1 KINGS 18:41–46

In this exciting story, although there was a drought and a famine, Elijah had the faith to say, "I hear something. There is a sound of heavy rain." In the natural, there wasn't anything that told him rain was coming. There was no visible evidence of the clouds changing or the wind shifting or *any* change in the atmosphere that would have indicated an impending rainstorm. There was nothing in the natural that would have given Elijah any inkling that there was going to be a rainstorm. Other than his spoken word, "There is a sound of a heavy rain," there was no reason to believe that rain was coming.

In his spirit, perhaps Elijah heard something. Or perhaps he desired an ending to this drought, so he climbed to the top of Mount Carmel, bent down to the ground, and began to pray. Regardless, seven times he told his servant to go back and look, go back and look, go back and look.

How many times do you think *you* would have told the servant to go back? After three or four times, most people would probably have said, "Oh, there isn't any rain," or "I guess I heard wrong," or "There's nothing happening," and then given up. But Elijah continued, over and over and over and over and over and over. Seven times he went back to find the evidence of what he had been praying about.

It is important to take note of this particular passage because many people give up long before it's time. They don't remain persistent or continue to look for the blessings of what God is doing in their atmosphere. Even if the evidence is as small as it was in this passage—a cloud as small as a man's hand—continue to look for the answer to your prayer. Remember, this tiny cloud rapidly developed into the massive rainstorm that Elijah had heard in his spirit.

It is so important to speak into your atmosphere and *continue* to speak, to not give up no matter what you see and no matter what people may be saying. When you hear people remark, "Hey, *this* is not going to happen," or "*That's* not going to happen," it's important for you to say, "No, it's not over until God says so," and keep checking to see if what you've been praying for is actually beginning to manifest. Don't be moved by what you see or by other people's opinions.

Now let's look at James 3:2–12:

We all stumble in many ways. If anyone is never at fault in what he says, he is a perfect man, able to keep his whole body in check.

When we put bits into the mouths of horses to make them obey us, we can turn the whole animal. Or take ships as an example. Although they are so large and are driven by strong winds, they are steered by a very small rudder wherever the pilot wants to go. Likewise the tongue is a small part of the body, but it makes great boasts. Consider what a great forest is set on fire by a small spark. The tongue also is a fire, a world of evil among the parts of the body. It corrupts the whole person, sets the whole course of his life on fire, and is itself set on fire by hell.

All kinds of animals, birds, reptiles and creatures of the sea are being tamed and have been tamed by man, but no man can tame the tongue. It is a restless evil, full of deadly poison.

With the tongue we praise our Lord and Father, and with it we curse men, who have been made in God's likeness. Out of the same mouth come praise and cursing. My brothers, this should not be. Can both fresh water and salt water flow from the same spring? My brothers, can a fig tree bear olives, or a grapevine bear figs? Neither can a salt spring produce fresh water.

Being an experienced horse trainer and equestrian, I understand what James means regarding the use of a bit to steer the entire horse. You can actually make this twelve-hundred-plus-pound animal stop dead in its tracks just by using the correct bit. By applying the right pressure to that bit, you can turn its body completely around. You can make it go to the left or to the right. With the proper bit, you have full control of the entire animal. It's quite enlightening to see the numerous types of bits and equipment that you can put into a horse's mouth or over its face in order to make it submit. Submission is *the* key component of obedience.

That being said, it's very important that you bridle your own mouth in such a way that it will produce only words that are good. This may take practice for some of you who have come out of toxic households or struggle with toxic thoughts. Please note, however, that the Scriptures declare that "the mouth speaks what the heart is full of" (Luke 6:45). It is crucial, therefore, that you learn not to speak mindless words or random words and thoughts. Additionally, never agree with or accept someone else's negative words spoken about you, your circumstance, or your situation. You have the right to reject what you know is not God's best for you.

Unfortunately, many times our words create an atmosphere around us that is toxic. The Bible calls it poison. We can actually speak words of poison into our lives. We can speak a negative atmosphere into existence with our tongue.

We can curse someone, or we can even curse ourselves.

Sometimes people have a tendency to just *want* to speak, but as we have discovered, you *will* eat the fruit of your words. It's very important to be deliberate about the words you say and to make up your mind not to say anything at all if you can't say something good. Never speak out of anger. Don't be quick to have a smart answer for someone, and don't decide that you're just going to say whatever you want because that's how you feel at the time. That's exactly what can bind you up, block your blessings, or even arrest your blessings.

One way to determine if your words might be arresting your blessings is to commit to keeping a word journal. For an entire week, jot down your favorite "sayings," and keep a record of the conversations you have with the people in your life (your spouse, your children, your coworkers, and others). You may also want to keep a journal of your thoughts during that same week. At the end of the week, go back and read your journal. You might be very surprised by what you read, and you might even need to detox your thoughts as well as your words.

I've heard it said that you should watch your thoughts because they become your words. Watch your words because they become your actions. Watch your actions because they become your habits. Watch your habits because they become your character. And watch your character because it becomes your destiny. I agree with that whole-heartedly, and I believe you will find it true for your life as well.

Lastly, meditate on Proverbs 13:3: "Those who guard their lips preserve their lives, but those who speak rashly will come to ruin." Make up your mind to create an atmosphere and a life of blessings by using words filled with faith and victory. Get into the habit of never speaking death or defeat, no matter what your circumstances look like or feel like. When you begin to realize the power of your spoken words, your atmosphere will begin manifesting all of God's promises. Never ever give up—ever!

Life Talk
Key #3 - Words of Confession

"You are what you eat". Proverbs 18:21 tells us that we will eat the fruit of our words, and I have watched many people suffer because they wouldn't harness their mouths. I have repeatedly seen many people fall victim to speaking curses upon their lives, especially when their emotions are running high. It is often easy to lash out or speak irrationally when a situation presents itself that causes fear. A bad report at the doctor, the sudden loss of a job, the breakup of a marriage or relationship, family strife, and the list goes on and on.

*I have experienced three monumental, terrifying health scares in my family that allowed me to see the power of prayer and God's Word in action. As a believer, we can take our authority over certain situations. We should get into the habit of understanding that our spoken word- aligned with our faith (belief in what **God** says about the situation) - creates MIRACLES. These family medical reports*

53

included: a severed artery with a complete loss of blood and the need to be transfused repeatedly in order to sustain life, stage-four cancer with positive readings in the lymph nodes, and West Nile virus which the vet said would leave neurological damage and very possibly death. It would have been very easy for me to break down and have a "hysterics moment". It would have been easy for me to "expect" death since that is what all three situations pointed at. It would have been easy for me to get mad at God for "allowing" these things to happen and for allowing the doctors to be incompetent and not careful in their practice. However, I am fortunate enough to understand that we will have what we say we will have, and we have a God who cannot lie! His Word is His bond, and He is able to do all things except fail. His Word is our instruction manual, and if we follow it and rely on it, we can live full and blessed lives. When Jesus cursed the fig tree, and his disciples were amazed that it stopped bearing fruit, He told them, "I tell you the truth, if you have faith and do not doubt, not only can you do what was done to the fig tree, but also you can say to this mountain, 'Go, throw yourself into the sea,' and it will be done. If you believe, you will receive whatever you ask for in prayer."(Matthew 21:21-22). When I hear a negative report, I begin to tell the situation to wither and die (Matthew 21:18). I speak TO it, not about it (Matthew 21: 21-22). It is important to understand the instructions that Jesus left for us! HE said, "If you BELIEVE, you will RECEIVE whatever you ask for in prayer." I have seen miracles in eleventh-hour situations by praying what He said to pray, and not letting my feelings dictate what words come out of my mouth!

I am sure that you noticed my comment about West Nile virus, and the comments that the vet made. Many people do not believe in praying for their pets or animals, but I do. And I've seen it work! I understand that God is concerned for and about me. This includes the things that He has entrusted to me for care and enjoyment. When my horse was diagnosed suddenly with the virus, I was informed that because she wasn't young, she probably had a better chance of beating it, but that she would most likely suffer from neurological damage. I was devastated since this was my trusted competition mount and companion of 9 years. I asked the Lord to show me how to deal with this in His Word, and I found Deuteronomy 28. In it, the Scriptures tell us what blessings are ours when we are obedient to the Lord which included my barns, my livestock, and the fruit of my livestock. It includes everything I put my hand to. I was to be blessed in the city, and blessed in the country (Deut. 28:1-11)! Since West Nile was not a blessing, I told it where to go as I declared and decreed God's Word about the situation. The vet said he had never seen a horse recuperate so quickly (she only spent 7 days with him!). Two years later, she gave birth to a beautiful filly on Easter morning, thus confirming that the fruit of my livestock shall be blessed! I must mention here that several horses in my county died from the disease so I had every reason to feel like I was going to lose her, but when I allowed my faith to be stirred up and my actions to align with God's Word, I received a miracle! Friends, please don't underestimate the power of releasing God's Word into your atmosphere and your life! You have the power of life and death in your tongue. CHOOSE LIFE!

Key #4

Oaths and Pledges

We have learned that our tongues hold life or death, and I want to use that lesson to illustrate another way that many believers have arrested their blessings without understanding what has taken place. Many congregations and televangelists teach that believers should combine a monetary gift with their prayer petitions. These gifts are often called "sacrificial offerings" or "seed offerings." It is taught that the believers are making a sacrifice in order to substantiate the seriousness of their petitions. Or sometimes it is said that the money represents a release of something in the natural in order to gain something spiritual.

Quite frequently in these instances, 1 Kings 17 is quoted as a reference. The prophet Elijah and the widow woman are cited as the biblical text examples for receiving unending provision when you give your last to the man (or woman) of God. I firmly believe in giving and making sure that the righteous person or prophet is rewarded (see Matthew 10:40–42); however, it is important to understand what adding money to a prayer request effectually does.

For the record, I want to clearly state that I believe it is important to give to the Kingdom in order to spread the good news. I also believe that we receive rewards and blessings when we are a blessing to others. However, here is where the issue lies: when we add money to our prayer requests or petitions, we are making a pledge, and that sets in motion certain consequences. Let me explain.

Dictionary.com defines *pledge* as "something delivered as security for the payment of a debt or fulfillment of a promise and subject to forfeiture on failure to pay or fulfill the promise." Another definition says "a hostage"! Pledging money that is tied to a prayer request means you are essentially entering into a binding agreement, with your prayer request as the collateral. What happens when you fail to make payments on your car or your home? It gets repossessed or foreclosed, right? A similar thing happens in the spirit realm when you make a pledge that you do not keep.

The Bible warns us several times not to make a pledge and then fail to fulfill it. The same holds true of a vow. A *vow* is defined as "a solemn promise or statement; especially one by which a person is bound to an act, service, or condition" (Dictionary.com). Wow! Do you see how serious this is?

Many times the person who is initiating these monetary pledges will say, "Just pay as you can. Do what you can do, and the Lord will do what He can do." Or they might urge, "Pay a little something each month: five dollars, ten dollars, whatever you can give." Now most people are fired up when they first make their pledges. They sincerely want to give it all. The believers with the biggest hearts are the ones who want to be involved in all the activities going on within their congregations, so they often make pledges to the building fund, missionaries, the new school, or whatever.

Christian television networks need more money to put more satellites up in order to broadcast the message of our Lord and Savior, Jesus Christ, so they ask for pledges and donations. Some faith healers ask you to "sow a seed" into their ministries as they pray for your healing or the healing of a loved one. These seeds vary in amount, and sometimes believers will pledge large amounts, if their need is great. Thousand-dollar pledges are not uncommon.

Here is the pitfall that traps and arrests the blessings in all these examples: If you make a pledge and then only pay as you can—five or ten dollars each month—it becomes easier with each passing month to forget about the pledge as life gets in the way. Eventually, you stop paying on it, and ultimately, you forget about it. But guess who hasn't forgotten? God! And the collateral—your prayer request—is just sitting out there unable to be fulfilled because you did not fulfill your end of the agreement. God is waiting for you to finish your pledge or do what you promised (vowed) in order to release your blessing.

Take time to carefully read and reread Ecclesiastes 5:1–7. While this instruction may seem harsh, we now know the devastating effects of careless words, as well as the danger of unpaid vows and pledges:

Guard your steps when you go to the house of God. Go near to listen rather than to offer the sacrifice of fools, who do not know that they do wrong.

Do not be quick with your mouth, do not be hasty in your heart to utter anything before God. God is in heaven and you are on earth, so let your words be few. A dream comes when there are many cares, and many words mark the speech of a fool.

When you make a vow to God, do not delay to fulfill it. He has no pleasure in fools; fulfill your vow. It is better not to make a vow than to make one and not fulfill it. Do not let your mouth lead you into sin. And do not protest to the temple messenger, "My vow was a mistake." Why should God be angry at what you say and destroy the work of your hands? Much dreaming and many words are meaningless. Therefore fear God.

Let's also look at Jonah. He was sitting in the belly of a great fish when he prayed this prayer:

From inside the fish Jonah prayed to the Lord his God. He said:

"In my distress I called to the LORD, and he answered me. From deep in the realm of the dead I called for help, and you listened to my cry. You hurled me into the depths, into the very heart of the seas, and the currents swirled about me; all your waves and breakers swept over me. I said, 'I have been banished from your sight; yet I will look again toward your holy temple.' The engulfing waters threatened me, the deep surrounded me; seaweed has wrapped around my head. To the roots of the mountains I sank down; the earth beneath barred me in forever. But you, LORD my God, brought my life up from the pit.

"When my life was ebbing away, I remembered you, LORD, and my prayer rose to you, to your holy temple. Those who cling to worthless idols turn away from God's love for them. But I, with shouts of grateful praise, will sacrifice to you. What I have vowed I will make good. I will say, 'Salvation comes from the LORD.' " And the LORD commanded the fish, and it vomited Jonah onto dry land.

—JONAH 2

Jonah was vomited onto dry land after he prayed to the Lord and said he would make good on his vow. If you have a monetary vow or pledge that needs to be repaid, please repent as Jonah did, and then get it paid. Unlock your blessings!

Another man worth taking note of is Job. Job was a man of God who was tested mightily and won his battle as he stood in faith—even when his wife and friends advised otherwise. Let's look in Job 22:

Submit to God and be at peace with him; in this way prosperity will come to you. Accept instruction from his mouth and lay up his words in your heart.

If you return to the Almighty, you will be restored: If you remove wickedness far from your tent and assign your nuggets to the dust, your gold of Ophir to the rocks in the ravines, then the Almighty will be your gold, the choicest silver for you. Surely then you will find delight in the Almighty and will lift up your face to God. You will pray to him, and he will hear you, and you will fulfill your vows. What you decide on will be done, and light will shine on your ways.

—JOB 22:21–28

Submitting to God and being at peace with Him allows prosperity to come to you. When you walk according to His Word and instruction, blessings and favor will be granted to you. Notice that verses 23–28 of Job 22 tell us how to be restored. And as part of our restoration, He will answer our prayers, and *we* will fulfill our vows. "What you decide on will be done, and light will shine on your ways." Wow, light and blessings—this is the way to live!

For the record, I have made vows and pledges and have learned the hard way what happens when you forget to fulfill your end of the agreement. I have nothing negative to say about making monetary pledges or vows. I just want you to be aware of your duty to God before you enter such an agreement. It is a very serious transaction, and many people are suffering greatly because of forgotten pledges.

Another type of binding agreement is an oath. *To make an oath* is defined as "to swear solemnly; to vow" (Dictionary.com). Many people will add an oath to their prayer petition without understanding its effect. They will say something like "Lord, I swear I will _____ or_____ if You will do _____"; or "Lord, I promise to do _____ if You will do _____."

This seems innocent enough until the person praying gives up after a few days or weeks when it doesn't look as though an answer is coming. Remember, a delay doesn't necessarily mean a denial. Sometimes the Lord is orchestrating some things, and time will have to pass before the blessing arrives.

Nevertheless, the spoken oath binds the promise to the prayer request, so it is imperative for the person to do what was promised in order to receive the blessing. Be cautious, therefore, about your words.

Before I end this chapter, I want to briefly touch on oaths in other settings. Sometimes people join organizations, secret societies, or fraternities and sororities that require them to make a verbal pledge or oath prior to their acceptance into the group. Though I know many Christians who belong to these types of organizations, I want to remind you that our God is a jealous God and does not permit us to pledge our allegiance to anyone other than Him. Please take this into consideration if you have a noticeable hindrance in your life that began shortly after you took an oath to an organization or club.

It is a serious matter to the Lord when you pledge your honor and duty to someone or something other than Him or His will for your life. He despises idols and pride, and many times a person's rank and order in these organizations can take on the image of an idol as duty and responsibility increase. Please understand that I am not categorically against joining these types of organizations. I have many strong, Christian friends who belong to them, but I am warning you about the words of your mouth and the fruit that it produces. If you put anything before God—your career, your spouse, your children, your social status, your bank account, or anything else—it is considered an idol, and God does not deal lightly with these issues. Be aware of the things you are saying and doing!

Life Talk

Key #4 - Unpaid Pledges and Vows

Because of the way things had rapidly diminished in my finances, I was desperate for direction from God. I was attending a weekly prayer meeting and one of the women there began to share with me how she went through a similar time in her life. She shared the book of Jonah with me and how two things brought him to the belly of the whale: running away from God's instruction and unpaid vows. She said that her finances overflowed once she paid back some forgotten pledges.

I went home that night and began to ask God to remind me of any and all pledges and/or vows that I had made but had forgotten. Eventually it came to mind! There was televangelist that I followed for many years until his program went off the air. I had pledged money to his ministry and had stopped paying it. By using the internet, I was able to find the phone number of the ministry. A quick call to them revealed the balance that had remained for over ten years! I quickly paid the bal-

ance and within two weeks, I received a job offer with the county. I had been looking for work for eleven months and after I paid my pledge, the job offer came! It was a full-time professional job with medical and dental benefits. Hallelujah!

Key #5

Unforgiveness

I have saved this key for last because it is often the hardest to overcome. Unforgiveness is a huge blockage for most believers because it creates a barricade that prevents their blessings from getting to them. Forgiveness is the most powerful concept to embrace, because once you have mastered the principle of forgiveness, the enemy will not be able to keep you bound. You will be released and ready to receive your blessings as well as be a true blessing to others.

Let us start with how Jesus instructed His disciples (which includes you and me) to pray: "Our Father in heaven, hallowed be Your name. Your kingdom come, Your will be done on earth as it in heaven. Give us today our daily bread. Forgive us our debts as we also have forgiven our debtors, and lead us not into temptation, but deliver us from the evil one" (Matt. 6:9–13).

Jesus then went on to give extremely crucial instruction in verses 14 and 15: "For if you forgive men when they sin against you, your heavenly Father will also forgive you. But if you do not forgive men their sins, your Father will not forgive your sins."

Most people are familiar with the Lord's Prayer, which is Matthew 6:9–13, but the following two verses are rarely taught. However, this is an area that can most definitely arrest your blessings. Ignoring these two verses can hold back what God desires to give you. Plainly said, if you don't forgive, then He cannot forgive you, which ties His hands. It is important to deeply meditate on this and make a decision today that you will forgive.

Many people don't want to forgive because they don't quite understand what it truly means. Allow me to explain what it means and what it does not mean, and then we can talk about the Scriptures that really help us to see God's big picture concerning this issue.

First of all, *forgive* is a verb. It is something you do, not just something you discuss or think about. It requires action on your part. According to the *World English Dictionary, to forgive* means "to cease to blame or hold resentment against; to grant pardon for a mistake or wrongdoing; to free or pardon someone from penalty; and to free from the obligation of" (Dictionary.com). In other words, when you make the decision to forgive, it means you cease to blame *and* you cease to hold resentment against the one who hurt you. It means that you grant a pardon for the mistake or wrongdoing that was done to you and that you also agree to free—or pardon—the offender from any penalties caused by the offense. This means the person does not have to repay you for anything he or she has done, and you completely release the offender from the obligation to pay you back. Ultimately, forgiveness means that you completely let it go, and neither party owes the other *anything.*

Letting go of an offense and the resentment that goes along with it does not mean that you're required to reconcile with that individual, that group, or whoever the offender may be. Forgiveness *does not* mean reconciliation, nor does it mean that you have to trust that person or that group or organization. Trust and reconciliation are not part of forgiveness at all. With this in mind, we can see that forgiveness is simply about letting go of the offense, letting go of the resentment, and letting go of the blame.

I know this is a big pill to swallow, but God is asking us to do it because, by doing this, we free our spirits from harboring bitterness. Bitterness will produce the wrong fruit in our lives, and that fruit can rob us of our blessings. With bitterness and unforgiveness in our hearts, we become angry, fearful, and obnoxious to be around because we're harboring hurts from the past. We *have* to learn how to stop blaming and holding resentment against others and move forward with our lives.

The Bible teaches that whatsoever we bind on earth is bound in heaven, and whatsoever we loose on earth is loosed in heaven (Matt. 18:18). Evangelist and author Liberty Savard has written several prayers using this particular Scripture to help believers loose themselves from the effects of their past. She teaches about binding our minds, our hands, our hearts, and our feet to the will and purposes of God, and loosing ourselves from the negative effects, feelings, and emotions of past events so that they're not trapped in our souls. For more information on this topic, please study her books *Shattering Your Strongholds* and *Breaking the Power: Of Unmet Needs, Unhealed Hurts, Unresolved Issues in Your Life. Shattering Your Strongholds* teaches what strongholds are and how they keep us bound (Savard, 1993), while *Breaking the Power* teaches how to manage and heal the unsurrendered soul (Savard, 1997).

In my opinion, unforgiveness is an emotional (and spiritual) tether that keeps us tied to the offender. The last place most people would ever want to be is tied to the person that hurt them, but that's exactly what unforgiveness does. Unforgiveness keeps us bound and unable to receive our blessings; therefore, in prayer, bind yourself to the will and purposes of God, and loose yourself from all wrong mind-sets, erroneous thoughts, destructive habits, bad attitudes, and misguided emotions in order to stabilize your heart(i.e. emotions) and be set free (Savard, 1993, 1997).

Let's take a look at Psalm 103:8–12. This Scripture passage clearly shows that God wants to forgive us: "The Lord is compassionate and gracious, slow to anger, abounding in love. He will not always accuse, nor will He harbor His anger forever; he does not treat us as our sins deserve or repay us according to our iniquities. For as high as the heavens are above the earth, so great is his love for those who fear him. As far as the east is from the west, so far has he removed our transgressions from us." The word *transgressions* means sinful acts.

This is such a beautiful Scripture because it shows us that God doesn't treat us as our sins deserve or repay us according to our iniquities. Therefore, if we are created in His image and likeness (Gen. 1:26–27), then we have the ability to do the same towards other people. We do not have to repay them for what they have done to us. We don't have to give them what they deserve.

We can ask the Lord to help us learn how to forgive and gain victory in our lives over this issue. He only asks for the desire to forgive to be there so that He can do the rest. Remember, it's not through our own might that we are able to do this, but only through His Spirit and His power.

Are you struggling in the area of forgiving yourself? Sometimes it's easier to forgive other people than it is to forgive yourself. But forgiving yourself is an important key to unlocking the blessings that God is trying to give you. Forgiving yourself does not include beating yourself up or feeling continually guilty about something that happened that was not in line with God's Word. It is also not right for you to try to make up for whatever you did through works or deeds as a repayment for that sin. Only the blood of Jesus has the power to wash away sin in your life—not your works or deeds.

Hebrews 10:15–18 says, "The Holy Spirit also testifies to us about this. First, he says: 'This is the covenant I will make with them after that time, says the Lord. I will put my laws in their hearts and I will write them on their minds.' Then he adds: 'Their sins and lawless acts **I will remember no more**, and *where these have been forgiven, <u>sacrifice for sin is no longer necessary</u>.'* (emphasis mine).

According to that Scripture, "Where these have been forgiven, sacrifice for sin is no longer necessary" (Heb. 10:18), your confession of the sin and sincere expression of sorrow are all that God requires. No other atonement through a man or through a religious ceremony has to happen, and carrying guilt is not part of the forgiveness-of-self process either. Just confess your sin to the Lord. Say you're sorry, and then don't go back to it. That's all He expects you to do. However, He also requires that you extend that same open-hand, open-heart action to those who have offended you.

I believe this is *the* most important lesson of your life to learn: to forgive. Forgiveness means (1) to forgive the offense; (2) to forgive, or let go of, the feelings that were attached to the offense; and (3) to never forget the lesson attached to the event. It's important to remember the lesson of the event so that you don't repeat it again or find yourself continually trapped in a self-destructive cycle.

Let's ask ourselves a few more questions where forgiveness is concerned. If you're finding it hard to forgive someone, ask yourself the following:

1. How do I benefit by holding onto the past?

It's important to understand there is no benefit in the past. The past is over with. It's done. There's nothing you can do about it. There is nothing that you can fix or change. There is nothing that you can salvage. It's over with. It's gone. The only thing that you have is today, and the only thing you can hope for is tomorrow. But as far as yesterday, it's over and it's done.

Remember what the Lord told Lot when he and his family were leaving Sodom and Gomorrah: not to look back. But Lot's wife did look back, and she turned into a pillar of salt (Gen. 19:26). That tells you that there is nothing good about looking back at a place God is delivering you from (a bad marriage, an addiction, bad habits, a job, a location, etc.).

This is especially true if you are trying to get even for an offense or be vindicated in some form or fashion. Allow the Lord to vindicate you. Do not go back into a situation that wasn't God's will for your life. It's just best to let it go. Remember, there will always be a consequence for your behavior and your actions. You will always reap what you sow (Galatians 6:7).

2. *Who really pays for my unwillingness to forgive?*

Do you think that the person who offended you is really paying for anything? He or she is probably not even thinking about you or remembers you or understands that you're still thinking about something that happened however long ago. You're the one that's going to suffer by being unwilling to forgive!

3. *What is the lesson for me to learn?*

There's always going to be a lesson to learn, and as long as you learn it, that's your reward. It's not about getting even. Understand that the Lord said vengeance is His (Rom. 12:19–21). Allow Him to be your vindicator. You need to move forward with your life so that you can receive all the blessings and favor He desires you to have. And though I believe forgiveness is a choice, I do not believe it is an option. It is absolutely necessary that you forgive in order to receive the fullness of everything that God has for you.

Life Talk

Key #5 - Forgiveness

I have experienced many painful relationships in the past. Numerous counts of rejection and a painful divorce haunted me for many, many years. Rejection and abandonment work in tandem to rob you of your self-esteem and self-confidence.

I was devastated after my divorce because I had been deeply betrayed during a series of events that played themselves out like a horrific nightmare—only I was wide awake! I was unable to comprehend how the people who were supposed to love and protect me could reject me at my most vulnerable time. The pain of rejection eventually grew into bitterness and, once that bitterness took root, it manifested in several different ways. I developed a very strong independent spirit that drove me to build a wall around myself. I became a workaholic and enjoyed being immersed in the fruit of my labor. My life revolved around me, and therefore I began to develop roots of pride. I convinced myself that I didn't really need anyone and that if I chose to keep anyone around, it would be on my terms and for my benefit. This continued for years.

Fortunately, the Lord had other plans, and He led me to my weekly prayer meetings. These meetings were full of deliverance and prophecy, and I would continue to ask God to help me let go of the past because it was tormenting me and driving me to become someone I didn't necessarily like. Over time—about a year—I was able to let go of some of the bitterness. I had to get very serious about making forgiveness a part of my life. I read several books about forgiveness, overcoming betrayal, overcoming my "Judas", and learning to trust again. My bookshelves are full of those topics! It did not happen overnight, but I believe that because I had made up my mind to press ahead and not look back, God released me from the memories of the feelings that being rejected and betrayed gave me. While I clearly remember several painful and negative events, I no longer have any emotions tied to them. I can honestly say that I was able to live out my deliverance and am no longer haunted by the emotional trauma caused by being wounded by loved ones.

It is important to remember that forgiveness is not a free pass to allow people to mistreat or abuse you. You are not obligated to trust or reconcile with the offender. However, you must let go of the offense and not expect any repayment from the offender. Let God be your vindicator! He can do things that no man can possibly do for you! And He knows just how to bring your situation to full justice. By pursuing a love walk and remaining diligent about Jesus' command to forgive, you will be releasing a multitude of blessings on your life. Once I truly forgave—not "just put it behind me" —I felt the heavy loads and burdens lift off of my life. I had been carrying those spiritual weights for too long! I felt such a relief and a peace that I hadn't known before. My entire being benefitted from me letting go of those offenses: my complexion cleared up, I had more energy, and I even lost a few pounds! Forgiveness is entirely about benefitting you—not the offender!

A Final Thought

Above all else, understand that God truly loves you. He desires nothing more than to bless you abundantly in your health, in your finances, in your relationships, as well as in your job satisfaction. You name it, and He wants you to have the very best of it!

Always remember that you are blessed in order to be a blessing. The more you share, the more He can funnel through your hands. These keys will help unlock some of the things that may have been withheld from you.

Sometimes God's will for your life may not align with what you are asking for. In that case, He will guide you to the path He desires you to follow if you will seek His face. At other times, the timing for your request may not be right, so pray for contentment (not patience!) during your waiting period. Praying for patience will generally produce trials for you to overcome, since that is the only way to learn how to be patient, so I am specifically using the word *contentment* here.

Abraham and Sarah waited more than twenty years for Isaac's birth. Be sure to keep in mind that a delay does not necessarily mean a denial. God may be trying to prepare you or the situation so that He gets the glory from it. He will not bless a mess, so pay attention to your atmosphere and your living habits. He is a God of order. He may be waiting on you to complete some things He has instructed you to do before He can do His part. Pay attention!

God may also be taking you through a maturing process so that you will be able to handle the blessing He has in store for you. If you are not mature, you may squander or waste it. He knows exactly what and how much we can handle, so He is not in any hurry to give us something prematurely and risk hindering our walk with Him. We cannot expect blessings if they end up becoming distractions or entanglements. Being able to successfully manage a blessing is a qualification for receiving more.

I pray that you will continue to seek God and His will in all things and that you understand that His love for you is greater than anything that you could comprehend or imagine. Know that even if you make mistakes, God is willing to forgive you and wants to immediately bring you back to Himself. He is able to make any crooked paths straight.

I pray that this book has been a blessing to you and that it may have revealed some places that you can now identify and correct so that your harvest of blessings can come in quickly. Be blessed. Your best is yet to come!

APPENDIX

Scripture references used throughout the book

Scripture references for Key #1

Hebrews 11:6

And without faith it is impossible to please God, because anyone who comes to him must believe that he exists and that he rewards those who earnestly seek him.

Hebrews 11:1

Now faith is being sure of what we hope for and certain of what we do not see.

Matthew 7:24-27

Therefore everyone who hears these words of mine and puts them into practice is like a wise man who built his house on the rock. The rain came down, the streams rose, and the winds blew and beat against that house; yet it did not fall, because it had its foundation on the rock. But everyone who hears these words of mine and does not put them into practice is like a foolish man who built his house on sand. The rain came down, the streams rose, and the winds blew and beat against that house, and it fell with a great crash.

Galatians 6:7-8

Do not be deceived: God cannot be mocked. A man reaps what he sows. The one who sows to please his sinful nature, from that nature will reap destruction; the one who sows to please the Spirit, from the Spirit will reap eternal life.

Ecclesiastes 3:1-8

A Time for Everything
There is a time for everything,
    and a season for every activity under heaven:
a time to be born and a time to die,
    a time to plant and a time to uproot,
a time to kill and a time to heal,

a time to tear down and a time to build,
a time to weep and a time to laugh,
a time to mourn and a time to dance,
a time to scatter stones and a time to gather them,
a time to embrace and a time to refrain,
a time to search and a time to give up,
a time to keep and a time to throw away,
a time to tear and a time to mend,
a time to be silent and a time to speak,
a time to love and a time to hate,
a time for war and a time for peace.

Genesis 18

The Three Visitors

The LORD appeared to Abraham near the great trees of Mamre while he was sitting at the entrance to his tent in the heat of the day. Abraham looked up and saw three men standing nearby. When he saw them, he hurried from the entrance of his tent to meet them and bowed low to the ground. He said, "If I have found favor in your eyes, my lord, do not pass your servant by. Let a little water be brought, and then you may all wash your feet and rest under this tree. Let me get you something to eat, so you can be refreshed and then go on your way—now that you have come to your servant." "Very well," they answered, "do as you say." So Abraham hurried into the tent to Sarah. "Quick," he said, "get three seahs of fine flour and knead it and bake some bread." Then he ran to the herd and selected a choice, tender calf and gave it to a servant, who hurried to prepare it. He then brought some curds and milk and the calf that had been prepared, and set these before them. While they ate, he stood near them under a tree. "Where is your wife Sarah?" they asked him. "There, in the tent," he said. Then the LORD said, "I will surely return to you about this time next year, and Sarah your wife will have a son." Now Sarah was listening at the entrance to the tent, which was behind him. Abraham and Sarah were already old and well advanced in years, and Sarah was past the age of childbearing. So Sarah laughed to herself as she thought, "After I am worn out and my master is old, will I now have this pleasure?" Then the LORD said to Abraham,

"Why did Sarah laugh and say, 'Will I really have a child, now that I am old?' Is anything too hard for the LORD? I will return to you at the appointed time next year and Sarah will have a son." Sarah was afraid, so she lied and said, "I did not laugh." But he said, "Yes, you did laugh."

Abraham Pleads for Sodom

When the men got up to leave, they looked down toward Sodom, and Abraham walked along with them to see them on their way. Then the LORD said, "Shall I hide from Abraham what I am about to do? Abraham will surely become a great and powerful nation, and all nations on earth will be blessed through him. For I have chosen him, so that he will direct his children and his household after him to keep the way of the LORD by doing what is right and just, so that the LORD will bring about for Abraham what he has promised him." Then the LORD said, "The outcry against Sodom and Gomorrah is so great and their sin so grievous that I will go down and see if what they have done is as bad as the outcry that has reached me. If not, I will know." The men turned away and went toward Sodom, but Abraham remained standing before the LORD.[e] Then Abraham approached him and said: "Will you sweep away the righteous with the wicked? What if there are fifty righteous people in the city? Will you really sweep it away and not spare the place for the sake of the fifty righteous people in it? Far be it from you to do such a thing—to kill the righteous with the wicked, treating the righteous and the wicked alike. Far be it from you! Will not the Judge of all the earth do right?" The LORD said, "If I find fifty righteous people in the city of Sodom, I will spare the whole place for their sake." Then Abraham spoke up again: "Now that I have been so bold as to speak to the Lord, though I am nothing but dust and ashes, what if the number of the righteous is five less than fifty? Will you destroy the whole city because of five people?" "If I find forty-five there," he said, "I will not destroy it." Once again he spoke to him, "What if only forty are found there?" He said, "For the sake of forty, I will not do it." Then he said, "May the Lord not be angry, but let me speak. What if only thirty can be found there?" He answered, "I will not do it if I find thirty there." Abraham said, "Now that I have been so bold as to speak to the Lord, what if only twenty can be found there?" He said, "For the sake of twenty, I will not destroy it." Then he said, "May the Lord not be angry, but let me speak just once more. What if only ten can be found there?" He answered, "For the sake of ten, I will not destroy it." When the LORD had finished speaking with Abraham, he left, and Abraham returned home.

Hebrews 10:36-37

You need to persevere so that when you have done the will of God, you will receive what he has promised. For in just a very little while, "He who is coming will come and will not delay."

3 John 1:2, KJV

Beloved, I wish above all things that thou mayest prosper and be in health, even as thy soul prospereth.

James 2:17

In the same way, faith by itself, if it is not accompanied by action, is dead.

James 2:14-26

What good is it, my brothers, if a man claims to have faith but has no deeds? Can such faith save him? Suppose a brother or sister is without clothes and daily food. If one of you says to him, "Go, I wish you well; keep warm and well fed," but does nothing about his physical needs, what good is it? In the same way, faith by itself, if it is not accompanied by action, is dead. But someone will say, "You have faith; I have deeds." Show me your faith without deeds, and I will show you my faith by what I do. You believe that there is one God. Good! Even the demons believe that—and shudder. You foolish man, do you want evidence that faith without deeds is useless? Was not our ancestor Abraham considered righteous for what he did when he offered his son Isaac on the altar? You see that his faith and his actions were working together, and his faith was made complete by what he did. And the Scripture was fulfilled that says, "Abraham believed God, and it was credited to him as righteousness," and he was called God's friend. You see that a person is justified by what he does and not by faith alone. In the same way, was not even Rahab the prostitute considered righteous for what she did when she gave lodging to the spies and sent them off in a different direction? As the body without the spirit is dead, so faith without deeds is dead.

Deuteronomy 8:17-19

You may say to yourself, "My power and the strength of my hands have produced this wealth for me." But remember the LORD your God, for it is he who gives you the ability to produce wealth, and so confirms his covenant, which he swore to your forefathers, as it is today. If you ever forget the LORD your God and follow other gods and worship and bow down to them, I testify against you today that you will surely be destroyed.

Daniel 4:19-24

Then Daniel (also called Belteshazzar) was greatly perplexed for a time, and his thoughts terrified him. So the king said, "Belteshazzar, do not let the dream or its meaning alarm you."

Belteshazzar answered, "My lord, if only the dream applied to your enemies and its meaning to your adversaries! The tree you saw, which grew large and strong, with its top touching the sky, visible to the whole earth, with beautiful leaves and abundant fruit, providing food for all, giving shelter to the beasts of the field, and having nesting places in its branches for the birds of the air—you, O king, are that tree! You have become great and strong; your greatness has grown until it reaches the sky, and your dominion extends to distant parts of the earth.

"You, O king, saw a messenger, a holy one, coming down from heaven and saying, 'Cut down the tree and destroy it, but leave the stump, bound with iron and bronze, in the grass of the field, while its roots remain in the ground. Let him be drenched with the dew of heaven; let him live like the wild animals, until seven times pass by for him.'

"This is the interpretation, O king, and this is the decree the Most High has issued against my lord the king."

Daniel 4:28-37

All this happened to King Nebuchadnezzar. Twelve months later, as the king was walking on the roof of the royal palace of Babylon, he said, "Is not this the great Babylon I have built as the royal residence, by my mighty power and for the glory of my majesty?" The words were still on his lips when a voice came from heaven, "This is what is decreed for you, King Nebuchadnezzar: Your royal authority has been taken from you. You will be driven away from people and will live with the wild animals; you will eat grass like cattle. Seven times will pass by for you until you acknowledge that the Most High is sovereign over the kingdoms of men and gives them to anyone he wishes." Immediately what had been said about Nebuchadnezzar was fulfilled. He was driven away from people and ate grass like cattle. His body was drenched with the dew of heaven until his hair grew like the feathers of an eagle and his nails like the claws of a bird. At the end of that time, I, Nebuchadnezzar, raised my eyes toward heaven, and my sanity was restored. Then I praised the Most High; I honored and glorified him who lives forever. His dominion is an eternal dominion; his kingdom endures from generation to generation. All the peoples of the earth are regarded as nothing. He does as he pleases with the powers of heaven and the peoples of the earth. No one can hold back his hand or say to him: "What have you done?" At the same time that my sanity was restored, my honor and splendor were returned to me for the glory of my kingdom. My advisers and nobles sought me out, and I was restored to my throne and became even greater than before. Now I, Nebuchadnezzar, praise and exalt and glorify the King of heaven, because everything he does is right and all his ways are just. And those who walk in pride he is able to humble.

Philippians 4:6-9

Do not be anxious about anything, but in every-thing, by prayer and petition, with thanksgiving, present your requests to God. And the peace of God, which transcends all understanding, will guard your hearts and your minds in Christ Jesus. Finally, brothers, whatever is true, whatever is noble, whatever is right, whatever is pure, what-ever is lovely, whatever is admirable—if anything is excellent or praiseworthy—think about such things. Whatever you have learned or received or heard from me, or seen in me—put it into prac-tice. And the God of peace will be with you.

Scripture References for Key #2

Deuteronomy 28

Blessings for Obedience

If you fully obey the LORD your God and care-fully follow all his commands I give you today, the LORD your God will set you high above all the nations on earth. All these blessings will come upon you and accompany you if you obey the LORD your God:

You will be blessed in the city and blessed in the country.

The fruit of your womb will be blessed, and the crops of your land and the young of your livestock—the calves of your herds and the lambs of your flocks.

Your basket and your kneading trough will be blessed.

You will be blessed when you come in and blessed when you go out.

The LORD will grant that the enemies who rise up against you will be defeated before you. They will come at you from one direction but flee from you in seven.

The LORD will send a blessing on your barns and on everything you put your hand to. The LORD your God will bless you in the land he is giving you.

The LORD will establish you as his holy people, as he promised you on oath, if you keep the commands of the LORD your God and walk in his ways. Then all the peoples on earth will see that you are called by the name of the LORD, and they will fear you. The LORD will grant you abundant prosperity—in the fruit of your womb, the young of your livestock and the crops of your ground—in the land he swore to your forefathers to give you. The LORD will open the heavens, the storehouse of his bounty, to send rain on your land in season and to bless all the work of your hands. You will lend to many nations but will borrow from none. The LORD will make you the head, not the tail. If you pay attention to the commands of the LORD your God that I give you this day and carefully follow them, you will always be at the top, never at the bottom. Do not turn aside from any of the commands I give you today, to the right or to the left, following other gods and serving them.

Joshua 1:9

Have I not commanded you? Be strong and coura-geous. Do not be terrified; do not be discouraged, for the LORD your God will be with you wherever you go."

Exodus 6:6-9

"Therefore, say to the Israelites: 'I am the LORD, and I will bring you out from under the yoke of the Egyptians. I will free you from being slaves to them, and I will redeem you with an outstretched arm and with mighty acts of judgment. I will take you as my own people, and I will be your God. Then you will know that I am the LORD your God, who brought you out from under the yoke of the Egyptians. And I will bring you to the land I swore with uplifted hand to give to Abraham, to Isaac and to Jacob. I will give it to you as a possession. I am the LORD.'"

Moses reported this to the Israelites, but they did not listen to him because of their discouragement and harsh labor.

Exodus 16

The whole Israelite community set out from Elim and came to the Desert of Sin, which is between Elim and Sinai, on the fifteenth day of the second month after they had come out of Egypt. In the desert the whole community grumbled against

Moses and Aaron. The Israelites said to them, "If only we had died by the LORD's hand in Egypt! There we sat around pots of meat and ate all the food we wanted, but you have brought us out into this desert to starve this entire assembly to death."

Then the LORD said to Moses, "I will rain down bread from heaven for you. The people are to go out each day and gather enough for that day. In this way I will test them and see whether they will follow my instructions. On the sixth day they are to prepare what they bring in, and that is to be twice as much as they gather on the other days."

So Moses and Aaron said to all the Israelites, "In the evening you will know that it was the LORD who brought you out of Egypt, and in the morning you will see the glory of the LORD, because he has heard your grumbling against him. Who are we, that you should grumble against us?" Moses also said, "You will know that it was the LORD when he gives you meat to eat in the evening and all the bread you want in the morning, because he has heard your grumbling against him. Who are we? You are not grumbling against us, but against the LORD."

Then Moses told Aaron, "Say to the entire Israelite community, 'Come before the LORD, for he has heard your grumbling.'"

While Aaron was speaking to the whole Israelite community, they looked toward the desert, and there was the glory of the LORD appearing in the cloud.

The LORD said to Moses, "I have heard the grumbling of the Israelites. Tell them, 'At twilight you will eat meat, and in the morning you will be filled with bread. Then you will know that I am the LORD your God.'"

That evening quail came and covered the camp, and in the morning there was a layer of dew around the camp. When the dew was gone, thin flakes like frost on the ground appeared on the desert floor. When the Israelites saw it, they said to each other, "What is it?" For they did not know what it was.

Moses said to them, "It is the bread the LORD has given you to eat. This is what the LORD has commanded: 'Each one is to gather as much as he needs. Take an omer for each person you have in your tent.'"

The Israelites did as they were told; some gathered much, some little. And when they measured it by the omer, he who gathered much did not have too much, and he who gathered little did not have too little. Each one gathered as much as he needed.

Then Moses said to them, "No one is to keep any of it until morning."

However, some of them paid no attention to Moses; they kept part of it until morning, but it was full of maggots and began to smell. So Moses was angry with them.

Each morning everyone gathered as much as he needed, and when the sun grew hot, it melted away. On the sixth day, they gathered twice as much—two omers for each person—and the leaders of the community came and reported this to Moses. He said to them, "This is what the LORD commanded: 'Tomorrow is to be a day of rest, a holy Sabbath to the LORD. So bake what you want to bake and boil what you want to boil. Save whatever is left and keep it until morning.'"

So they saved it until morning, as Moses commanded, and it did not stink or get maggots in it. "Eat it today," Moses said, "because today is a Sabbath to the LORD. You will not find any of it on the ground today. Six days you are to gather it, but on the seventh day, the Sabbath, there will not be any."

Nevertheless, some of the people went out on the seventh day to gather it, but they found none. Then the LORD said to Moses, "How long will you refuse to keep my commands and my instructions? Bear in mind that the LORD has given you the Sabbath; that is why on the sixth day he gives you bread for two days. Everyone is to stay where he is on the seventh day; no one is to go out." So the people rested on the seventh day.

The people of Israel called the bread manna. It was white like coriander seed and tasted like wafers made with honey. Moses said, "This is what the LORD has commanded: 'Take an omer of manna and keep it for the generations to come, so they can see the bread I gave you to eat in the desert when I brought you out of Egypt.'"

So Moses said to Aaron, "Take a jar and put an omer of manna in it. Then place it before the LORD to be kept for the generations to come."

As the LORD commanded Moses, Aaron put the manna in front of the Testimony, that it might be kept. The Israelites ate manna forty years, until they came to a land that was settled; they ate manna until they reached the border of Canaan. (An omer is one tenth of an ephah.)

1 Samuel 15:22

But Samuel replied:

"Does the LORD delight in burnt offerings and sacrifices as much as in obeying the voice of the LORD?

To obey is better than sacrifice,

and to heed is better than the fat of rams."

Scripture References for Key #3

Proverbs 18:21

The tongue has the power of life and death,

   and those who love it will eat its fruit.

Hebrews 10:23

Let us hold unswervingly to the hope we profess,

for he who promised is faithful.

Luke 6:45

The good man brings good things out of the good stored up in his heart, and the evil man brings evil things out of the evil stored up in his heart. For the mouth speaks what the heart is full of.

1 Kings 18:41-45

And Elijah said to Ahab, "Go, eat and drink, for there is the sound of a heavy rain." So Ahab went off to eat and drink, but Elijah climbed to the top of Carmel, bent down to the ground and put his face between his knees.

"Go and look toward the sea," he told his servant.
And he went up and looked.

"There is nothing there," he said.

Seven times Elijah said, "Go back."

The seventh time the servant reported, "A cloud as small as a man's hand is rising from the sea."

So Elijah said, "Go and tell Ahab, 'Hitch up your chariot and go down before the rain stops you.'"

Meanwhile, the sky grew black with clouds, the wind rose, a heavy rain came on and Ahab rode off to Jezreel.

James 3:2-12

We all stumble in many ways. If anyone is never at fault in what he says, he is a perfect man, able to keep his whole body in check.

When we put bits into the mouths of horses to make them obey us, we can turn the whole animal. Or take ships as an example. Although they are so large and are driven by strong winds, they are steered by a very small rudder wherever the pilot wants to go. Likewise the tongue is a small part of the body, but it makes great boasts.

Consider what a great forest is set on fire by a small spark. The tongue also is a fire, a world of evil among the parts of the body. It corrupts the whole person, sets the whole course of his life on fire, and is itself set on fire by hell.

All kinds of animals, birds, reptiles and creatures of the sea are being tamed and have been tamed by man, but no man can tame the tongue. It is a restless evil, full of deadly poison.

With the tongue we praise our Lord and Father, and with it we curse men, who have been made in God's likeness. Out of the same mouth come praise and cursing. My brothers, this should not be. Can both fresh water and salt water flow from the same spring? My brothers, can a fig tree bear olives, or a grapevine bear figs? Neither can a salt spring produce fresh water.

Proverbs 13:3

He who guards his lips guards his life,

but he who speaks rashly will come to ruin.

Scripture References for Key #4

1 Kings 17

Then the word of the LORD came to him: "Go at once to Zarephath of Sidon and stay there. I have commanded a widow in that place to supply you with food." So he went to Zarephath. When he came to the town gate, a widow was there gathering sticks. He called to her and asked, "Would you bring me a little water in a jar so I may have a drink?" As she was going to get it, he called, "And bring me, please, a piece of bread."

"As surely as the LORD your God lives," she replied, "I don't have any bread—only a handful of flour in a jar and a little oil in a jug. I am gathering a few sticks to take home and make a meal for myself and my son, that we may eat it—and die."

Elijah said to her, "Don't be afraid. Go home and do as you have said. But first make a small cake of bread for me from what you have and bring it to me, and then make something for yourself and your son. For this is what the LORD, the God of

Israel, says: 'The jar of flour will not be used up and the jug of oil will not run dry until the day the LORD gives rain on the land.'"

She went away and did as Elijah had told her. So there was food every day for Elijah and for the woman and her family. For the jar of flour was not used up and the jug of oil did not run dry, in keeping with the word of the LORD spoken by Elijah.

Matthew 10:40-42

"He who receives you receives me, and he who receives me receives the one who sent me. Anyone who receives a prophet because he is a prophet will receive a prophet's reward, and anyone who receives a righteous man because he is a righteous man will receive a righteous man's reward. And if anyone gives even a cup of cold water to one of these little ones because he is my disciple, I tell you the truth, he will certainly not lose his reward."

Jonah 2

From inside the fish Jonah prayed to the LORD
his God. He said:

"In my distress I called to the LORD,

and he answered me.

From the depths of the grave I called for help,

and you listened to my cry.

You hurled me into the deep,

into the very heart of the seas,

and the currents swirled about me;

all your waves and breakers

swept over me.

I said, 'I have been banished

from your sight;

yet I will look again

toward your holy temple.'

The engulfing waters threatened me,

the deep surrounded me;

seaweed was wrapped around my head.

To the roots of the mountains I sank down;

the earth beneath barred me in forever.

But you brought my life up from the pit,

O LORD my God.

"When my life was ebbing away,

   I remembered you, LORD,

and my prayer rose to you,

   to your holy temple.

"Those who cling to worthless idols

   forfeit the grace that could be theirs.

But I, with a song of thanksgiving,

   will sacrifice to you.

What I have vowed I will make good.

   Salvation comes from the LORD."

And the LORD commanded the fish, and it vomited Jonah onto dry land.

Ecclesiastes 5:1-7

Fulfill Your Vow to God

Guard your steps when you go to the house of God. Go near to listen rather than to offer the sacrifice of fools, who do not know that they do wrong.

Do not be quick with your mouth,
    do not be hasty in your heart
    to utter anything before God.
God is in heaven
    and you are on earth,
    so let your words be few.
A dream comes when there are many cares,
    and many words mark the speech of a fool.

When you make a vow to God, do not delay to fulfill it. He has no pleasure in fools; fulfill your vow. It is better not to make a vow than to make one and not fulfill it. Do not let your mouth lead you into sin. And do not protest to the temple messenger, "My vow was a mistake." Why should God be angry at what you say and destroy the work of your hands? Much dreaming and many words are meaningless. Therefore fear God.

Job 22

Eliphaz

Then Eliphaz the Temanite replied:

"Can a man be of benefit to God?
Can even a wise man benefit him?
What pleasure would it give the Almighty if you
were righteous?
What would he gain if your ways were blameless?
"Is it for your piety that he rebukes you
and brings charges against you?
Is not your wickedness great?
Are not your sins endless?
You demanded security from your brothers for no
reason;
you stripped men of their clothing, leaving
them naked.
You gave no water to the weary
and you withheld food from the hungry,
though you were a powerful man, owning land—
an honored man, living on it.
And you sent widows away empty-handed
and broke the strength of the fatherless.

That is why snares are all around you,
   why sudden peril terrifies you,
why it is so dark you cannot see,
   and why a flood of water covers you.
"Is not God in the heights of heaven?
   And see how lofty are the highest stars!
Yet you say, 'What does God know?
   Does he judge through such darkness?
Thick clouds veil him, so he does not see us
   as he goes about in the vaulted heavens.'
Will you keep to the old path
   that evil men have trod?
They were carried off before their time,
   their foundations washed away by a flood.
They said to God, 'Leave us alone!
   What can the Almighty do to us?'
Yet it was he who filled their houses with good
things,
   so I stand aloof from the counsel of the wicked.
"The righteous see their ruin and rejoice;
   the innocent mock them, saying,
'Surely our foes are destroyed,
   and fire devours their wealth.'

"Submit to God and be at peace with him;
    in this way prosperity will come to you.
Accept instruction from his mouth
    and lay up his words in your heart.
If you return to the Almighty, you will be restored:
    If you remove wickedness far from your tent
and assign your nuggets to the dust,
    your gold of Ophir to the rocks in the ravines,
then the Almighty will be your gold,
    the choicest silver for you.
Surely then you will find delight in the Almighty
    and will lift up your face to God.
You will pray to him, and he will hear you,
    and you will fulfill your vows.
What you decide on will be done,
    and light will shine on your ways.
When men are brought low and you say, 'Lift them up!'
    then he will save the downcast.
He will deliver even one who is not innocent,
    who will be delivered through the cleanness of
    your hands."

Scripture References for Key #5

Matthew 6: 9-13

"This, then, is how you should pray:

'Our Father in heaven,

hallowed be your name,

your kingdom come,

your will be done

   on earth as it is in heaven.

Give us today our daily bread.

Forgive us our debts,

   as we also have forgiven our debtors.

And lead us not into temptation,

but deliver us from the evil one.'"

Psalm 103: 8-12

The LORD is compassionate and gracious,

   slow to anger, abounding in love.

He will not always accuse,

   nor will he harbor his anger forever;

he does not treat us as our sins deserve

   or repay us according to our iniquities.

For as high as the heavens are above the earth,

so great is his love for those who fear him;

as far as the east is from the west,

so far has he removed our transgressions from

us.

Hebrews 10:15-18

The Holy Spirit also testifies to us about this.

First he says:

"This is the covenant I will make with them

after that time, says the Lord.

I will put my laws in their hearts,

and I will write them on their minds."

Then he adds:

"Their sins and lawless acts

I will remember no more."

And where these have been forgiven, sacrifice for

sin is no longer necessary.

Genesis 19:17-26

As soon as they had brought them out, one of

them said, "Flee for your lives! Don't look back,

and don't stop anywhere in the plain! Flee to the mountains or you will be swept away!"

But Lot said to them, "No, my lords, please! Your servant has found favor in your eyes, and you have shown great kindness to me in sparing my life. But I can't flee to the mountains; this disaster will overtake me, and I'll die. Look, here is a town near enough to run to, and it is small. Let me flee to it—it is very small, isn't it? Then my life will be spared."

He said to him, "Very well, I will grant this request too; I will not overthrow the town you speak of. But flee there quickly, because I cannot do anything until you reach it." (That is why the town was called Zoar.)

By the time Lot reached Zoar, the sun had risen over the land. Then the LORD rained down burning sulfur on Sodom and Gomorrah—from the LORD out of the heavens. Thus he overthrew those cities and the entire plain, including all those living in the cities—and also the vegetation in the land. But Lot's wife looked back, and she became a pillar of salt.

References

"Arrest." *Dictionary.com Unabridged.* Random House, Inc. May 26, 2011. <Dictionary.com http://dictionary.reference.com/browse/arrest>.

"Blessing." *Dictionary.com Unabridged.* Random House, Inc. May 26, 2011. <Dictionary.com http://dictionary.reference.com/browse/blessing>.

"Earnestly." *Dictionary.com Unabridged.* Random House, Inc. May 26, 2011. <Dictionary.com http://dictionary.reference.com/browse/earnestly>.

"Favor." *Dictionary.com Unabridged.* Random House, Inc. May 26, 2011. <Dictionary.com http://dictionary.reference.com/browse/favor>.

"Forgive." *Collins English Dictionary—Complete & Unabridged,* 10th edition. HarperCollins Publishers. May 26, 2011. <Dictionary.com http://dictionary.reference.com/browse/forgive>.

King James Bible. Public domain.

"Pledge." *Dictionary.com Unabridged.* Random House, Inc. May 26, 2011. <Dictionary.com http://dictionary.reference.com/browse/pledge>.

"Power." *Collins English Dictionary—Complete & Unabridged,* 10th edition. HarperCollins Publishers. May 26, 2011. <Dictionary.com http://dictionary.reference.com/browse/power>.

Savard, Liberty. *Breaking the Power: Of Unmet Needs, Unhealed Hurts, Unresolved Issues in Your Life.* Alachua: Bridge-Logos, 1997.

Shattering Your Strongholds. Alachua: Bridge-Logos, 1993.

CPSIA information can be obtained at www.ICGtesting.com
Printed in the USA
LVOW08s0506130813

347530LV00001B/2/P